requiem for a typewriter

poems by Moss Rich

For Milly and Shula, my wife and daughter

Requiem for a Typewriter

In memory of my much respected, electric (pre-electronic)
Olivetti Lexicon typewriter

They told me, O. Lexicon, that you had typed your last.
They said you had no future now – you only had a past.
They said "Two hundred pounds, please," to send you back alive.
I wept as I remembered that you cost me twenty five.

O! The crashing of your carriage shunting left to re-position,
Your motor busy-buzzing while I groped for composition,
The chattering of your keys printing words so often flawed.
Where the hell's the rubber-outer – look! Still hanging by its cord.

Years have rolled, winds of change have gusted through the land,
Amstrad, Canon, Brother, Sharp – not one bought second hand.
Friend of my first creative days, you served me well and true.
When I light my candles, Lexicon, there'll be one there for you.

With acknowledgements to Heraclitus by W. J. Cory 1823–92

Daughter of Wenceslas

For R – a young lady from the Czech Republic in our literary group
who adds excellence to our discussions of English poetry

"Bring me food and bring me wine, bring me pine logs hither…"

Peasants are we from the frosts of the woodlands
Foraging warmth for our souls in the good lands
Shrouded in darkness our minds as our bodies
Groping the air to discover where god is.

Low bent in peasant-hood lost for encouragement
Peers none from the castle, bearing us nourishment?
Ah! Lifting our eyes to the skies to assist us
Sing the lord's praises, the angels have kissed us.

Here in the midst of us, none to escort her
In an aura of grace, it is Wenceslas' daughter!

As fine Thought is food for the senses she hastens
To bring us the finest from Fortnum and Mason's.
Tastefully packaged in wisdom her language is
Rich with the relish of smoked salmon sandwiches
With honoured-guest dishes from our day to feudal
Soup of red beetroot, with sauerkraut and strudel.
And the fragrance! The fragrance that makes the heart quicken
How wishful the bone, how tender the chicken
And picked from the vineyard with fingertip care
The sweetest of grapes from a notable year.

The food from the fridge that K. Wenceslas emptied
He shared with Joe Peasant with nothing exempted.
So too our dear mentor whose Thought-generosity
Is boundless yet never is marred by verbosity.
Unfailing she gives us the meanings of meanings
Great poets have penned where we have only gleanings.
Unfailing she sees it her God-given mission
Upholding beneficent Royal tradition.
As when King to commoner "M'sieu let me offer yer
This scrumptious peanut dreamt up by Escoffier"
And draining a glass of a vintage Chianti,
The King to our Joey, "M'sieu, votre Santé."

Daughter of Wenceslas, Princess Bohemia,
Vous êtes la crème de la crème, only creamier.

New Poems by Robert Graves, 1962
From the Public Library

Three times this book's been taken from the shelf
including my time, March of '88,
since first it won a space in '86.

Thin, scantly noticed, like a morning clerk
and millions others scuttling into work
identified by personal bus ticket,
important as a pip inside an orange,
happening to be seen by chance, not want.
Some eighty thousand readers in this town
(barring the cannot-readers) shared it thrice.

No, I'm not moaning… Let me make a point.
God bless the poets, Britain needs their brains.
They also serve who help give steady jobs
to papermakers, printers and librarians.

I Look Before and After

In the looming days of my dotage
I look back for my hubris
to my exuberant, earlier poems
– slick, spiky and sophisticated –
and give them once more
their friendly nod of approval.

And through my warm afterglow
I see a clear drawn image
of the Emperor Nero
with bright, mad, heavenward gaze
fiddling happily
on the deck of the Titanic
unconscious of the fact that
all that remains of his audience
is a disordered row of empty deck-chairs
and the sweet, swirling sound that surrounds him
is not the music of his own creating.

This was an apology to a member of my group upset by a tasteless doggerel
I recited at one of our meetings. I believe it was accepted as sincere penitence.

The Orkneys

For a friend who went there to paint

The grey, ferocious ocean
pounds on the silent shore,
and waves rush to thrash the beach
and the beach lies still for more,
and honest maidens anciently
wed fishermen and bore.

Here ruthless Norseman orgied
and seas of blood were shed,
They annoyed the ancient islanders
and painted whole towns red,
and honest maidens fearfully
hitched up their skirts and fled.

These isles the Vikings ravaged
where wicked deeds were done,
Norwegians gave to Scotland
in 1471
and honest maidens hoped that now
they'd had their fill of fun.

The Vikings and the Norsemen
have left the place in peace
and things no longer happen here
so nothing needn't cease.
Honest maids aren't bothered now
so the public don't increase.

Yet still the angry ocean
drives folk and isles apart,
and barrenness and solitude
have struck the Orkneys' heart.
Now gifted ladies paint the scene
on canvas works of art.

Their eyes drawn to the highest points
– the skyline no one reaches –
their gleam of human thinking gives
more light than a thousand speeches.
And the wilderness invades their art
as the art invades the beaches.

With brush-touch of tenderness
they soothe the cruel sea.
They clothe the solitudes and crags
with instant sympathy
which men with honey-tongues will sell
in Bond Street and Paree.

On Hearing of the Death of a Forgotten Cousin

This death's a stone flung into a startled pond,
the edge I stand on doesn't sense a ripple.

Yet, staring at the Nothing where it splashed
I see a picture of a wife bereft, shocked
and in turmoil. Memories surging up

changing as sunny waters change reflecting
    when clouds pass casually, or a breeze
        ruffles their vacant face

recall joint boyhood mischief
outings and squabbles and borrowings of pence
and sharing boys' discoveries of girls
and Uncle proudly pictured in his Morris Cowley
then changing schools and school caps
and the gradual distancing
and the rare weak handshakes at funerals and weddings.

Now, sunken memories stirring, float to the top,
Death, with a stone, has churned the Past to Life.

The Morris Cowley was the first British-made popular car.

Devaluation – The Human Reality

The pound in my pocket
is a pound in my pocket.
It doesn't diminish or grow –

while the tooth in my mouth
is much less of a tooth
than it was only one year ago.

Now the truth of the tooth
which was loose in its socket
if only yours truly could use it.

When I try to exchange it
for dollars or Francs
I'm met with a very wide
grin and "No Thanks!"

So the tooth, unemployed,
leaves an unhealthy void
and a man fills the socket
with pounds from my pocket.

Terminal Tragedy

She got off the train at Euston
One morning at five past nine
And she saw from the puddled platform
That the weather was far from fine.

She travelled all night from Glasgow
And passed Lancaster by
And had barely glimpsed that city
Through the dim of her sleepy eye.

Her terminus was Manchester
At break of early day
But alas for her daughter's meeting
The train didn't go that way.

A careworn, widowed figure
Her years beyond three score
But still she bore them bravely
And could shoulder several more.

This night her mind goes backwards
To the days when they were two
Now Sunday after Sunday
She sits in a lonely pew.

Past Crewe and past Nuneaton
Meanwhile speeds the train
Into the brick of Bedford
Into the slanting rain.

The buffet car is closed now
It has fulfilled its function
No chance of a tonic cup of tea
Till you're well past Watford Junction.

At last at Euston station
Tired-eyed and unalert
Her hand slips off the carriage door
Full of British Railway's dirt.

Beneath her feet a puddle
Will cause a fatal slip
And a sharp click of a breaking rib
Like the crack of a cowboy's whip.

In a pained, regretful moment
She knew she had been silly
She should have taken the stopping train
To Manchester Piccadilly.

She thought of the excess to pay
She thought of her pensioned purse
Thin as it was it was thinner now
And about five pounds the worse.

They took her off to Casualty
And laid her in bed seven
Which the matron thought convenient
As the corner nearest heaven.

She died at noon and never knew
It had rained that night in Manchester too.

Capital Transfer

Son, I've worked for fifty years, I've had me ups and downs.
And now me bank account is yours – it's plenty thousand pounds.

Dad, old boy you're great
I always knew that you had guts!

Son, I've worked for fifty years, me profitable game
Should legally be yours, and you can carry on the name.

Trust me, Dad, it's done tonight
Before the lawyer shuts.

Son, I've worked for fifty years, me vast experience
Is worth a little fortune – it's the stuff of common sense

I shall stuff it safely, father
Where the monkey stuffs his nuts.

**Transfers of capital are subject to tax in certain circumstances.
The term is much favoured by eager tax inspectors.**

Lament for a New Year

Our years-long battle with Life grows wearisome.

Our arms are over-stretched and out of date.
Our wavering fire falls short of target.

Our front line faculties are slow and sullen
and even mutinous –

and our supply lines clatter no longer –
there are no more Reserves.
Our teeth are voting with their feet.

Hoist the white flag – Cry "Halt – we've had enough!"

And remember to release the girls
imprisoned in our shrunken memories.

The Crime

It was done – it was done forever
Time allowed no return
A happening can't unhappen
A fire does not unburn.

And Memory has no doorman
The elite and the lout
Can equally gain entry
There's no fence says KEEP OUT!

Did you read of the Anschluss? My mother
Had a letter from Vienna one day
"Our dear son is no longer with us"
Was all it dared to say.

When a day's too dark for dawning –
– A dirge too sad to sing
Memory nudges a hidden hand
To pluck at a hidden string.

Not all our floods of all our tears
Can wash an eternal stain
We may dry our eyes for Abel
We shall ever remember Cain.

ANSCHLUSS:
The Nazi annexation of Austria in 1938 followed by notorious celebrations and tragedies in Vienna. It was a foretaste of the Holocaust to come.

The Art of Grief

Walking through the cemetery I keep stopping to stare at the letters on the tombstones. They suspend Grief – they are the Art of Grief.

If print speaks as gently to your heart as blood flows softly through your veins you will understand why I stop to read, and read again.

The lettering is simple, respectful, dry-eyed and in golden balance… a restrained sans serif as quiet on the white stone as anything Eric Gill ever put on paper for London Underground. And incised with an angel's delicacy…

To each of his valued clients the stonemason gives a generous package of his renewable stock of grief. He uses good, industrial Black and Decker and, for important commissions, a new quarter inch drill point.

When his own time comes to 'lay his tools to rest' he too will expect his fellow masons to apply their art in a manner consistent with their professional dignity and his family's munificence.

The National Cat Show

Here was the flower of the feline world,
the shapes, complexions, eyes, the skins
the very cream of British Moggidom.

Here too were the judges to shower the prizes
and we the people to applaud them all.
And choice among the champions
I saw one heart-stopper,
suave, elegant, and very, very vogue.
I smiled at IT – it noticed ME.
It puckered it's nostrils, gave a slight yawn
rose leisurely in its enclosure
and turned the other way.

With deeply felt indifference
it rose again,
stretched its soft form to a valley and gentle hills
and curled down once more to await the judgement.

All over its luxury
the judges hands wandered and pondered
and the pleasure on his face showed the purring in his heart.
I watched the virtuous creature lying on the bench
graciously acquiescent;
and it was then Eugenia Waddington-Sharpe
that I took to thinking so very, very, very warmly
of You.

Moths

My dressing gown was in decay
I bought a new one yesterday

It's made of nylon mixed with cotton
Design-wise we all think it's spot-on

This morning when I left my bed
I met a moth who sneering said

Mate, I'm leaving now, you fool
There is no substitute for wool."

Two Women

This one carries weights and falters
She finds her road a constant climb.
She didn't know when she started out
Some weights increase with time.

Her destination drags her onwards
Her load is live with urgent voice.
The home the road will lead her to
Is not the home of choice.

The other, too, once dragged her burdens.
Now freer in body and mind
She goes where purpose points the way
She's left her loads behind.

Which is the way to the Self Expressed?
The one, bemused, gropes forward-back
The other with spirit and eye alert
Skirts round the cul-de-sac.

Now and again they meet at pleasures.
One weary; brittle-smooth the other.
They clash, they do not understand –
these mothers – one another.

Conduct Unbecoming

Behaviour
is the offspring
of ambience.

You do not
in reverent amazement
shout out Holy Smoke!
at your rich aunt's cremation –
nor wash with runny tears
the Ming vase
you later find
she has bequeathed to you.

And IF,
all of a sudden
at Royal Ascot
you find yourself on the rim
outside the carefree, lightly clad
summery throng
then pushed inside the Royal Enclosure
you desist from patting the flanks
of thoroughbred fillies.

The View From the Eigth Floor Flat on the Sea Front

We live too high for mice, our crumbs
Don't tempt them up at night.
Our windows, washed by the public rain,
Are far from the public sight.
    And no one knocks down on our ceilings
    To say our radio jars their feelings
    For no one absolutely no one
    Lives here at a higher height.

The people in the ground floor flats
Have had a rate rebate.
The ground floor bar has got them
In a pretty nervous state.
    The foyer, once select and smart,
    Now holds convivial male and tart.
    At weekends, downstairs, no one
    Gets to sleep till it's very late.

We're very fond of our civilized
And elegant Life Design.
We breathe sweet air, we're friends with birds,
Our view of the sea is fine.
    The lofty state that we live in
    Is quite remote from common sin,
    And we don't know what goes on below
    So long as we're home by nine!

This poem was written in 1982. Since then the bar has been under the most respectable ownership.

Moss Rich: An Appreciation

I first met Moss Rich around 1990. He looked very like the dormouse at the Mad Hatter's Tea Party, except that he was awake. In fact, Moss is very wide awake indeed. He read some of my work. His critiques were polite, firm and devastatingly accurate.

This selection of Moss' work spans 20 years of writing from 1977–1997. Moss says he started writing poetry in the 1970s. But his wife Millie remembers him writing her love poems in the thirties. He also composed parodies of famous poems for ads in the forties and fifties, when he was Advertising Manager with the company that evolved into Travis Perkins. Moss has a sharp wit and a wicked sense of humour.

He was born in 1910 and showed early promise with a Distinction in English at Central Foundation School, London EC1. During the Second World War he spent time in the Army Pay Corps, but left as they couldn't provide him with strong enough lenses for his spectacles. On his journey as a poet he moved from Poetry Round in Earl's Court, London, to Brunswick Poets and Brighton Nightwriters in Brighton & Hove.

In 1975, Moss wrote a short satirical poem and sent it to Leapman, a leading diarist on The Times, who published it and sent Moss a cheque. Moss felt he was on to something and has continued to win prizes ever since, including a magnum of Champagne from The Independent's Limerick Competition.
He's been published in the Penguin Book of Limericks and numerous anthologies and magazines.

If every developing poet needs a mentor, then at a critical point in my own development, for a while Moss was mine. He always reminds me that poets and poems work best when they don't take themselves too seriously. So thanks Moss for your critical discernment and your encouragement.

Moss wrote almost all his poems to be recited in public. He played a part in the move of poetry from page to stage that has resulted in the many forms of performance poetry so enjoyed today. It's good to know the oral tradition is still very much alive.

As I write Moss is approaching 95 and still recites his verse from memory.
In spite of failing eyesight and hearing, his sense of humour, clarity of thought and lyrical gift remain undiminished.

John Davies
December 2005